SAVING the WORLD

FUSION

Making a Difference at SCHOOL

by
Hermione Redshaw

BEARPORT
PUBLISHING

Minneapolis, Minnesota

Credits: All images courtesy of Shutterstock.com. With thanks to Getty Images, Thinkstock Photo, and iStockphoto. Front Cover © GoodStudio, AnastasiaNi, Mari Dambi, GoodStudio. 2&3 © Walnut Bird. 4&5 © My Life Graphic, Refat. 6&7 © kali9, KittyVector, pingebat. 8&9 © EZ-Stock Studio, saaton, MicroOne. 10&11 © Monkey Business Images, SpeedKingz. 12&13 © iva, Shyntartanya, Real_life_Studio. 14&15 © Sunny studio, Robert Kneschke. 16&17 © Rawpixel.com, Dmytro Zinkevych, elenabsl. 18&19 © Africa Studio, New Africa, Ivan Dubovik. 20&21 © areetham, rawpixel.com. 22&23 © MIA Studio, Robert Kneschke, lakkana savaksuriyawong, Alinute Silzeviciute, BRO.vector.

Library of Congress Cataloging-in-Publication Data is available at www.loc.gov or upon request from the publisher.

ISBN: 979-8-88509-358-3 (hardcover)
ISBN: 979-8-88509-480-1 (paperback)
ISBN: 979-8-88509-595-2 (ebook)

For more information, write to Bearport Publishing, 5357 Penn Avenue South, Minneapolis, MN 55419.

CONTENTS

OUR HOME

At school, we can learn all about our **planet** and everything it does for us. Earth is our home, and we must take care of it.

There are many things you can do at school to help Earth. You can make a difference. Let's learn how to save the world at school!

Earth is home to about 8 billion people.

GOING TO SCHOOL

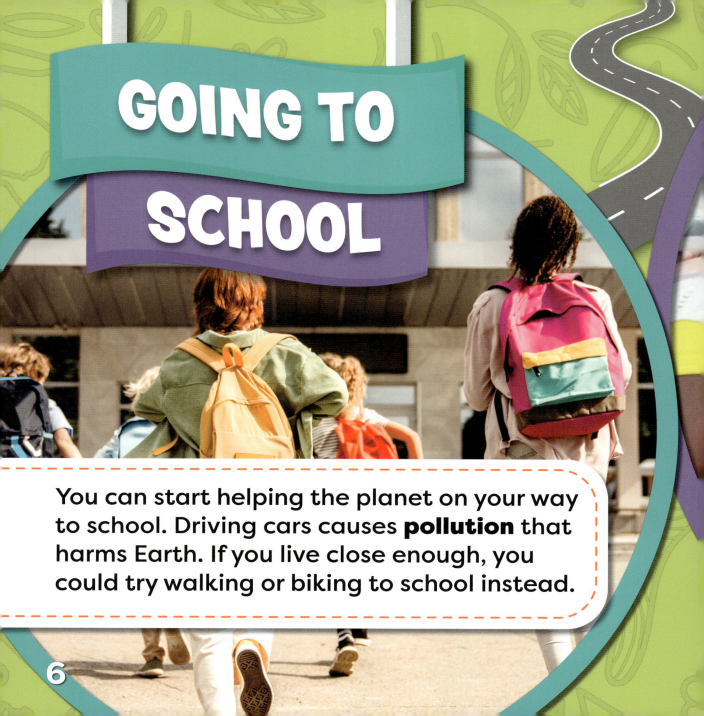

You can start helping the planet on your way to school. Driving cars causes **pollution** that harms Earth. If you live close enough, you could try walking or biking to school instead.

Taking a school bus or carpooling with friends helps, too. When you ride with others, there are fewer cars on the road.

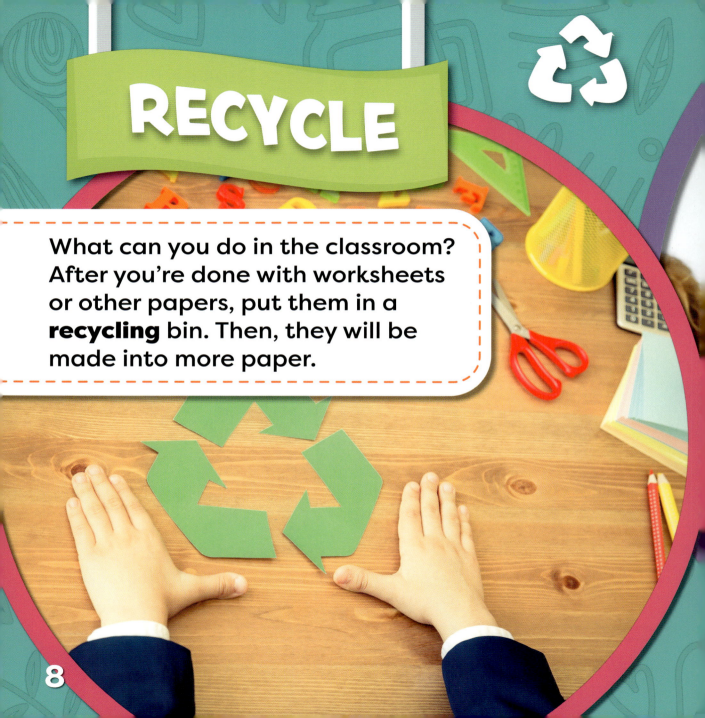

RECYCLE

What can you do in the classroom? After you're done with worksheets or other papers, put them in a **recycling** bin. Then, they will be made into more paper.

This helps save trees. Many trees are cut down to make new paper. But if more paper is made by recycling, then fewer trees are cut.

Many plastic, glass, and metal items can also be recycled.

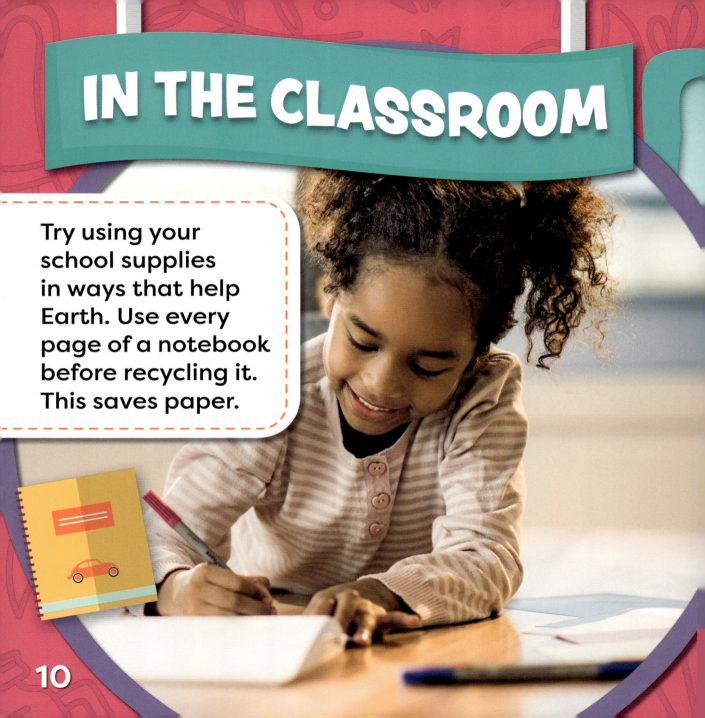

IN THE CLASSROOM

Try using your school supplies in ways that help Earth. Use every page of a notebook before recycling it. This saves paper.

Reusing things instead of throwing them away helps, too. You can reuse old cans or jars by decorating them to make pencil cups.

LUNCH TIME

If you bring a lunch to school, carry it in something you can reuse, such as a lunch box. **Single-use** items that you toss in trash cans go to **landfills**. All the trash piled up in landfills is bad for Earth.

Some paper bags are made from recycled paper.

If you do not have something reusable, try bringing a paper bag, which can be recycled.

13

MEAT-FREE LUNCHES

Think about what you are eating for lunch, too. A lot of meat comes from big farms that harm Earth. But you can help by eating less meat.

If your school serves meat-free lunches, give them a try. If not, you could ask your teachers about adding meat-free meals to the menu.

ORGANIZE EVENTS

Everyone at school can work together to help save the planet! Organize a **litter** pickup event with your classmates.

You can look for litter right outside your school building. This keeps the land clean.

DONATE TO CHARITY

A charity gives things to people who really need them.

You can also help the planet and people at your school by having a charity event. At the event, people can **donate** unwanted toys and clothes instead of throwing them away.

When you give things to a charity, they will be used by someone else who needs them. Donating helps people get what they need, and reusing things helps the planet.

SPEAK UP!

Some people may not know we need to help the planet. Others may not know what to do.

You can speak up to help people learn about Earth. If your school doesn't have a group trying to help the planet, ask to set one up.

CREATE A PLAN
OF ACTION

You can even make a plan for saving the planet! Ask your classmates to help you.

Think of things you can do to help Earth. Then, write them down. Here are some ideas to get you started . . .

Ask school about meat-free lunches.

Plan of Action

1. Recycle old homework papers.

2. Organize a class litter pickup.

3. Donate old clothes to a charity.

Reuse an old can to make a pencil cup.

Start a carpool.

GLOSSARY

donate to give something away to help others

landfills large holes in the ground used for dumping trash

litter trash that has been left on the ground

planet a large, round object that circles the sun

pollution harmful things being added to nature

recycling turning used things into new things

reusing using something again

single-use something that can be used only once before it must be thrown away or recycled

INDEX